Art Museum

Larry D. Thomas

Art Museums

Larry D. Thomas

Blue Horse Press
PO Box 7000 – 148 Redondo Beach, CA 90277
2014

Cover art: "The Menil Collection" (Houston, Texas) by Lisa P. Thomas

Editors: Jeffrey Alfier and Tobi Cogswell

ISBN-13: 978-0692252703

Other Poetry Collections by the Author

<u>Book-length Collections</u>

2001: *Amazing Grace* (poems), *Texas Review* Press, Huntsville, Texas

2004: *Where Skulls Speak Wind* (poems), *Texas Review* Press, Huntsville, Texas

2005: *Stark Beauty* (poems), Timberline Press, Fulton, Missouri

2008: *The Fraternity of Oblivion* (poems), Timberline Press, Fulton, Missouri

2008: *Larry D. Thomas: TCU Texas Poet Laureate Series* (poems), TCU Press, Ft. Worth, Texas

2010: *The Skin of Light* (poems), Dalton Publishing, Austin, Texas

2011: *A Murder of Crows* (poems), Virtual Artists Collective, Chicago, Illinois

2013: *Uncle Ernest* (poems), Virtual Artists Collective, Chicago, Illinois

2014: *The Lobsterman's Dream: (Poems of the Coast of Maine)*, El Grito del Lobo Press, Fulton, Missouri

Chapbooks

2001: *The Lighthouse Keeper* (poems),
Timberline Press, Fulton, Missouri
2002: *The Woodlanders* (poems), Pecan Grove
Press, San Antonio, Texas
2007: *With the Light of Apricots* (poems), Lily
Press
2007: *Eros* (poems), *Slow Trains Literary Journal*
2008: *The Circus* (poems), *Right Hand Pointing*
2009: *Plain Pine* (poems), *Right Hand Pointing*
2010: *Dark Pearls* (poems), LaNana Creek Press
(Stephen F. Austin State University),
        Nacogdoches, Texas
2010: *Wolves* (poems), El Grito del Lobo Press,
Fulton, Missouri
2010: *Five Lavender Minutes of an Afternoon*
(poems), *Right Hand Pointing*
2011: *The Red, Candle-lit Darkness* (poems), El
Grito del Lobo Press, Fulton, Missouri
2011: *Far (West Texas)* (poems), *Right Hand
Pointing*
2012: *Social Networks* (poems), *Right Hand
Pointing*
2013: *Colors* (poems), *Right Hand Pointing*
2014: *The Goatherd* (poems), Mouthfeel Press, El
Paso, Texas

for the Museum District of Houston, Texas,
in whose dappled shadows
I resided for twenty-four years

Acknowledgments

"The Docent," "The Restorer" and "Kimbell Art Museum" were first published in *DIN Magazine* (New Mexico State University).

"The Security Guard" first appeared in *Right Hand Pointing*.

"The Art Preparators" was first published in *Ruminate Magazine*.

"Museum of Fine Arts, Houston" first appeared in *Right Hand Pointing* with the title, "Art Museum."

"Mill Aluminum" (Epilogue), in a slightly different version, was first published in the *Cenizo Journal*, First Quarter, 2010; it also appeared in *The Skin of Light*, Dalton Publishing, 2010.

Cover Photo: "The Menil Collection" (Houston, Texas) by Lisa P. Thomas

Cover Design: Jeffrey C. Alfier and Tobi Cogswell

Table of Contents

Preface

I first visited the Chinati Foundation (contemporary art museum) in Marfa, Texas, approximately twenty years ago, and have subsequently enjoyed its offerings on numerous occasions. The museum is home to much of the work of the late Donald Judd, one of the most significant American artists of the post-war period, in addition to the work of several other artists whose work Judd admired.

During my first visit, while viewing and contemplating Judd's mill aluminum structures housed in two former artillery sheds of an old fort, I was struck by the seamless unity of artwork, the architecture of the museum housing it, and the large windows flooding the exhibition space with natural light and vistas of the high desert landscape surrounding it. The bright light and landscape vistas were dazzling in their interplay with the pristine, reflective surfaces of the aluminum, obliterating the traditional boundaries between artwork, exhibition space, landscape, and light. I noticed as I walked around each aluminum structure that its appearance kept changing with my movement, leaving me at times so taken with the light that my very "self" seemed merged with the radiant, epiphanic "oneness" of the experience. An ardent appreciator of visual art and a museum visitor for decades, I had never before experienced an art museum so one with art, space, landscape and light that each element was, at least perceptually, indistinguishable from the other three elements. This "dialogue" between a work of art and its exhibition space (including the personnel responsible for their preservation) has captivated my interest, artistic and otherwise, for decades, and, I trust, provided the crux for this series of poems.

One of the primary reasons Judd selected Marfa for his installations was his fascination with the light and undeveloped landscape of far West Texas. He was a passionate preserver of the natural environment, and went out of his way to refurbish existing buildings for his installations rather than mar the environment with new structures. Having been born and raised in West Texas, I have been privileged to enjoy a longstanding reverence for the natural beauty of the area, and have returned to it time and time again in much of my poetry.

Knowing Each Work

The Docent
(Museum of Modern Art, New York, New York)

When not bathing visitors
in the cadenced light
of his learning,

he follows them discreetly
as they navigate
the treacherous seas

of permanence.
For safety's sake,
he keeps them

behind the imaginary
bulletproof glass,
keeping sacrosanct

the pristine yard
between viewer eye
and canvas. He knows

the irreversible aftermath
visited on any viewer
too close to *Starry Night*.

The Security Guard
(The Menil Collection, Houston, Texas)

Every night, for decades,
he's had the whole place
to himself. He knows

each work with the intimacy
of close friendship, relishing
the impenetrable nuances

beyond the feeble reach
of his knowledge. Blind-
folded, he could identify

each canvas by its scent.
His sense of hearing
intensifies with each

passing night, alert
even to the soft collisions
of motes of dust. At times,

if he listens hard enough,
he can hear the slow,
deep breathing of the artists.

The Art Preparators
(Museum of Fine Arts, Boston, Massachusetts)

To ready masterworks
for an off-site exhibition,
they take deep breaths
prior to even touching
the frames. They treat

the deliberate gestures
of their fingers, snug
in latex gloves, as if
they were turning the frail
pages of the Gutenberg Bible.

They cherish the instruments
of their craft: the Oz Clips,
plastic wrap, tape, glass
for glazing, travel trays,
foam-lined storage crates,

and the intricacies
of moving and storing
the crates. Laboring
in the radiance of angels,
they secure the crates

gently in the temperature-
and-humidity-controlled
cargo space of the truck,
exhale their deep breaths,
drop to their knees, and pray.

The Restorer
(National Gallery of London, England)

As Ruhemann approached
the damaged masterwork*,
he cringed from the slashes
as if they ravaged
the flesh of his child.

Removing his raiment
of emotion and letting it
drop to his feet,
he freed his being
of every dangerous

microgram of feeling.
He invoked the passionless
god of knowledge
whose brain, saturate
with the sterile glow

of pure science,
creaked from a lifetime
of intimacy with oeuvre.
Before painstakingly
daubing each slash

with the first of countless
oil paints, he exchanged
his nerves, pupils, irises,
muscles, pulse, and breath
for Velázquez'.

* *The Toilet of Venus* ("The Rokeby Venus"), oil on
canvas by Diego Velázquez, 1647-51

The Sibilance of Shuffled Shoes

Museum of Fine Arts, Houston
(Houston, Texas)

The slightest
sound
is anathema:

this mausoleum:
hard wrought
residue

of whole lives,
hanging,
permanent:

crunched
to color,
line, shape,

texture:
executed
to perfection.

The Steps
(Philadelphia Museum of Art, Philadelphia, Pennsylvania)

The viewers
are ascending
the steps. Seventy-two
stone steps.

To weep
before *Sunflowers*;
to scale
the monumental

splendor of *The Large
Bathers*; to hear
the silence of *Three
Musicians*

playing a new way
of seeing *seeing*;
and to witness,
in perfect stillness,

the dizzying
motion of a *Nude
Descending
a Staircase*,

the viewers
are ascending
seventy-two
stone steps.

Art Museum of South Texas
(Corpus Christi, Texas)

Its shellcrete
periphery
is slapped

by the waves
of Corpus
Christi Bay.

*Blue Thrust**
bleeds on a wall
like an extra-

terrestrial craft,
disintegrating,
or a strange

undersea vessel
objectifying,
transparent

with stain
and opaque
with paint,

the cold fathoms
of blue
and being.

* oil on canvas by Dorothy Hood

All I Hear
(Walters Art Museum, Baltimore, Maryland)

is the sibilance
of shuffled
shoes.

The light,
deferent
with silence,

constricts
the pupils of eyes
to closed,

black nooses.
Noise
is restricted

to the chiseled
screaming
of color.

The floors
are gleaming
marble,

dignified
as the stone
of tombs.

Light Is Falling

Kimbell Art Museum
(Fort Worth, Texas)

Intrigued with the silver
aspect of Texas light,
the architect* abhorred
skylights and clerestory

windows. Natural light
enters through a two-
and-one-half-foot slit
at the apex of vaulted

ceilings; strikes convex,
perforated aluminum;
reflects onto curved
concrete; ricochets

off walls of travertine
and the warmth of an oak
floor; merges with light
from incandescent lamps;

and illumes, as if its oils
were still wet with freshness
and glowing from within,
La Tour's masterpiece**,

leaving the viewer complicit
in the dazzling trinity
of the cheat, the servant,
and the courtesan.

* Louis Kahn ** *The Cheat with the Ace of Clubs*

Amon Carter Museum
(Fort Worth, Texas)

From Maine, for its floors,
the architect* took tons of pink
and gray granite; for its walls:
shell stone, extruded bronze,
and Burmese teak. Its arched
and glass façade of timeless
classicism faces east, inhaling
cataracts of Texas sunlight.

In leaded zinc white, a painter**
found the moonlight; in Hooker
green, the ominous, elusive color
of darkness. Candlelit within,
jerked full speed down a hill
by six frantic, moon-blazed
horses, a stagecoach lunges
as if spewed from the night itself,
ejected from the canvas
into the trembling, outstretched arms
of the viewer.

* Philip Johnson

** *The Old Stagecoach of the Plains*
(oil on canvas by Frederic Remington)

Heading for the Higher Paying Jobs
(by Thornton Dial, High Museum of Art, Atlanta,
Georgia)

On canvas stretched taut
across wood: with oil, enamel,
wood, cloth, tin, wire screen,
and industrial sealing
compound, he labored.

Though technically untrained
in art, with the help of a Muse
hammered from the trappings
of hardened life, he divided
his masterwork into three
visual fields: a crude triangle
of cotton bolls burst open
in unforgiving yellow sunlight;
a violent, diagonal blue-black
dragged from the darkness
of iron and coal mines;
and a dominant trapezoid
crushing the fields below
with the red-hot
furnaces of a steel mill.
He stitched the fields together
with the sinuous whip
of the overseer.

(continued on next page)

It hangs for all time,
bathed in genteel radiance
filtered by a thousand
scoops of northern light.

Art Institute of Chicago, The Modern Wing
(Chicago, Illinois)

Light is falling.
Natural, northern light.
Light is falling
through the aluminum
blades of a "flying carpet."

Light is falling
to oil on a panel*
where a blind man,
clad in the tatters
of poverty, languors

in a dirge of blues.
The blind man is playing
a stringless guitar
he caresses like a warm,
brown angel. The light

of Piano** illumes
the browns of a guitar
in an ethereal duet,
holy with the promise
of warmth, music.

* *The Old Guitarist* (by Pablo Picasso)
** Renzo Piano, principal architect

Giant Boxes
(concrete works by Donald Judd, Chinati Foundation,
contemporary art museum, Marfa, Texas)

the size of small rooms,
of reinforced concrete,
are laid out on the desert
with the precision

of Egyptian pyramids.
The curator worked late,
into the evening, allowing me
to walk the path beside them.

The boxes were open,
occupied with the lavender
air of dusk, lavender
soon turning to black shadow

cast by a Comanche moon.
The wind, with unfettered
access to the boxes,
came and went as it pleased,

oblivious to my presence
as that of the rasping,
yellow grasses.
By the time I left,

the night had assumed
its residence there,
silent and deadly
as always.

Epilogue

Mill Aluminum
(untitled works by Donald Judd, Chinati Foundation,
contemporary art museum, Marfa, Texas)

The large windows
seemingly partitioning
the artwork from the landscape
are fashioned

of absolute clarity,
squared and quartered
with the stark
simplicity of angles

right as the natural,
palpable light
gloving the sheen
of mill aluminum

shimmering
with vistas
of blue mountains
and golden

seas of grass
where cattle graze
rapt in tongues
of reddish-brown fire

and landscape
melds with metal
in a seamless
dance of light.

About the Author

Larry D. Thomas, the 2008 Texas Poet Laureate and a member of the Texas Institute of Letters, has published several critically acclaimed collections of poems, most recently *The Lobsterman's Dream: Poems of the Coast of Maine* (El Grito del Lobo Press, Fulton, MO, 2014) and *The Goatherd* (Mouthfeel Press, El Paso, TX, 2014). Among the numerous awards and honors which he has received for his poetry are two *Texas Review* Poetry Prizes (2001 and 2004); the 2003 Western Heritage Award (Western Heritage Museum, Oklahoma); the 2004 Violet Crown Book Award (Writers' League of Texas); and selection as the 2002 Houston Area Barnes & Noble Booksellers Author of the Month. His *Larry D. Thomas: TCU Texas Poet Laureate Series* volume (TCU Press, 2008) was a semi-finalist for the National Book Award. Thomas's *As If Light Actually Matters: New & Selected Poems* is forthcoming from *Texas Review* Press (Texas A&M University Press Consortium) in 2015.